# THE WORLD BOOK

BLACKLINE
MASTERS
MAPS AND FLAGS

## FOR STATES AND PROVINCES

**Editorial:**       Shawn Brennan, Jeanne Johnson, Maureen Liebenson
**Cartography:**     Don Minnick, Wayne Pichler
**Art and Design:**  John Horvath, Wilma Stevens
**Production:**      Kathe Ellefsen, Madelyn Underwood, Jill Waltman
**Proofreading:**    Anne Dillon, Chad Rubel
**Manufacturing:**   Marco Morales

For information on other World Book products,
call 1-800-WORLDBK (967-5325), or visit our
Web site at **http://www.worldbook.com**.

World Book, Inc.
233 N. Michigan Ave.
Chicago, IL  60601

ISBN 0-7166-7402-5

Printed in the United States of America
1 2 3 4 5 6 7 8 9 06 05 04 03 02 01 00

# Table of Contents

15.00

# United

Scale bar for Alaska only

0          500 Miles

0          500 Kilometers

# States of America

## *"In God We Trust"*

Washington, D.C.

North

Scale bar for all states except Alaska

0               500 Miles

0          500 Kilometers

5

# U.S. Facts and Symbols

The United States flag includes 13 red and white stripes. In the upper-left corner are 50 white stars on a blue background. The stripes represent the original Thirteen Colonies. The stars represent the 50 U.S. states.

The bald eagle, a symbol of freedom and power, is found only in North America and is the national bird of the United States.

The Great Seal shows the bald eagle holding an olive branch and arrows, symbolizing a desire for peace but the ability to wage war. The reverse side bears the Eye of Providence, representing God, and a pyramid dated 1776, the year the U.S. declared its independence.

The United States of America is the third largest country in the world in population and the fourth largest in area.

The United States consists of 50 states and the District of Columbia. The District of Columbia is a piece of land set aside by the federal government for the nation's capital. The city of Washington covers the entire District.

**Front side of the Great Seal**

**Reverse side of the Great Seal**

# State Facts

| State | Area in sq. mi. | Area in sq. km | Admitted to the Union |
|---|---|---|---|
| Alabama | 51,718 | 133,950 | 1819 |
| Alaska | 587,878 | 1,522,596 | 1959 |
| Arizona | 114,007 | 295,276 | 1912 |
| Arkansas | 53,183 | 137,742 | 1836 |
| California | 158,648 | 410,896 | 1850 |
| Colorado | 104,100 | 269,618 | 1876 |
| Connecticut | 5,006 | 12,966 | 1788 |
| Delaware | 2,026 | 5,246 | 1787 |
| Florida | 58,681 | 151,982 | 1845 |
| Georgia | 58,930 | 152,627 | 1788 |
| Hawaii | 6,459 | 16,729 | 1959 |
| Idaho | 83,574 | 216,456 | 1890 |
| Illinois | 56,343 | 145,928 | 1818 |
| Indiana | 36,185 | 93,720 | 1816 |
| Iowa | 56,276 | 145,754 | 1846 |
| Kansas | 82,282 | 213,110 | 1861 |
| Kentucky | 40,411 | 104,665 | 1792 |
| Louisiana | 47,717 | 123,586 | 1812 |
| Maine | 33,128 | 85,801 | 1820 |
| Maryland | 10,455 | 27,077 | 1788 |
| Massachusetts | 8,262 | 21,398 | 1788 |
| Michigan | 58,513 | 151,548 | 1837 |
| Minnesota | 84,397 | 218,587 | 1858 |
| Mississippi | 47,695 | 123,530 | 1817 |
| Missouri | 69,709 | 180,546 | 1821 |

| State | Area in sq. mi. | Area in sq. km | Admitted to the Union |
|---|---|---|---|
| Montana | 147,047 | 380,849 | 1889 |
| Nebraska | 77,359 | 200,358 | 1867 |
| Nevada | 110,567 | 286,367 | 1864 |
| New Hampshire | 9,283 | 24,044 | 1788 |
| New Jersey | 7,790 | 20,175 | 1787 |
| New Mexico | 121,599 | 314,939 | 1912 |
| New York | 49,112 | 127,200 | 1788 |
| North Carolina | 52,672 | 136,421 | 1789 |
| North Dakota | 70,704 | 183,123 | 1889 |
| Ohio | 41,328 | 107,040 | 1803 |
| Oklahoma | 69,903 | 181,048 | 1907 |
| Oregon | 97,052 | 251,365 | 1859 |
| Pennsylvania | 45,310 | 117,351 | 1787 |
| Rhode Island | 1,213 | 3,142 | 1790 |
| South Carolina | 31,117 | 80,593 | 1788 |
| South Dakota | 77,122 | 199,744 | 1889 |
| Tennessee | 42,146 | 109,158 | 1796 |
| Texas | 266,874 | 691,201 | 1845 |
| Utah | 84,905 | 219,902 | 1896 |
| Vermont | 9,615 | 24,903 | 1791 |
| Virginia | 40,598 | 105,149 | 1788 |
| Washington | 68,126 | 176,446 | 1889 |
| West Virginia | 24,231 | 62,759 | 1863 |
| Wisconsin | 56,145 | 145,414 | 1848 |
| Wyoming | 97,818 | 253,349 | 1890 |

# Alabama

## *"We Dare Defend Our Rights"*

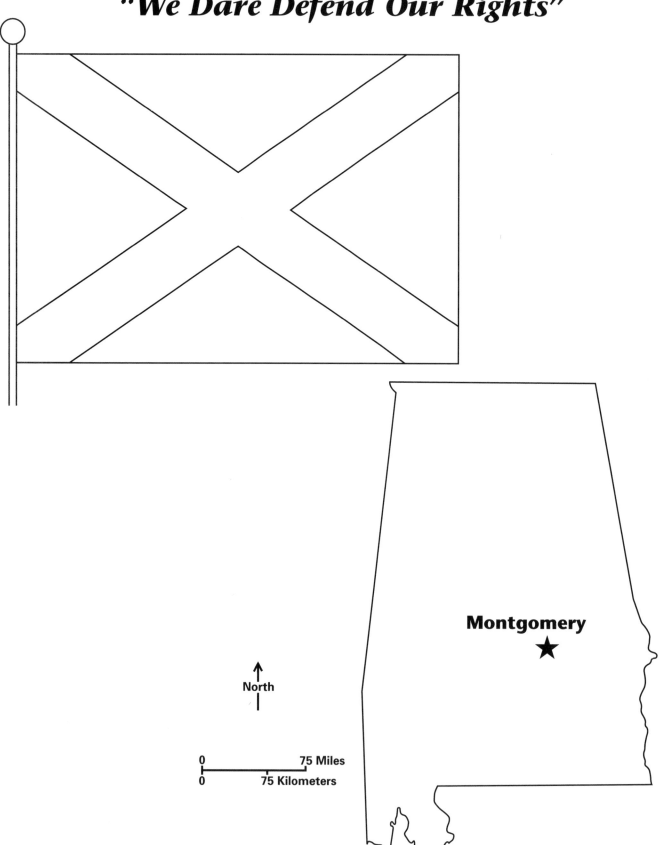

**Montgomery** ★

North

```
0              75 Miles
0        75 Kilometers
```

# Alaska

## *"North to the Future"*

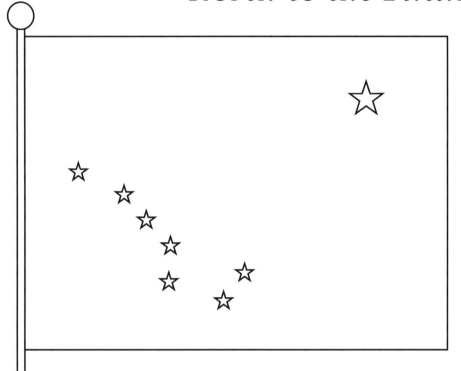

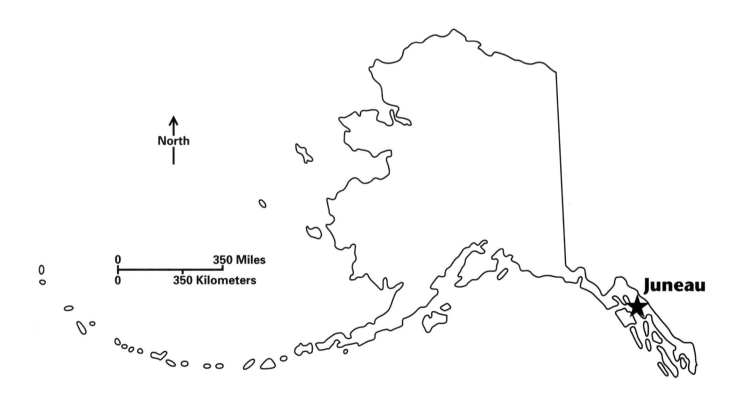

North

0        350 Miles
0        350 Kilometers

Juneau

# Arizona

*"God Enriches"*

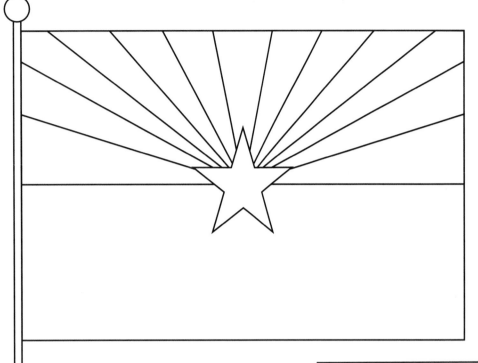

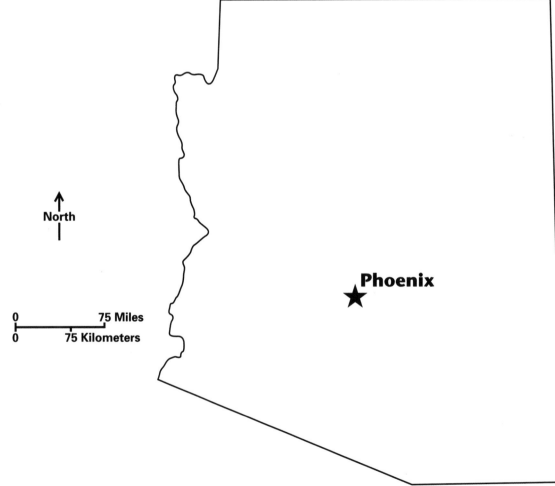

North

0       75 Miles
0       75 Kilometers

★ Phoenix

# Arkansas

## *"The People Rule"*

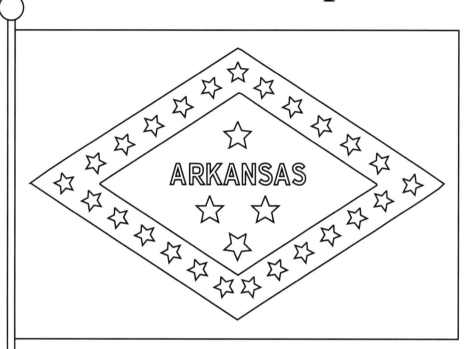

ARKANSAS

**Little Rock**
★

North

0       50 Miles

0       50 Kilometers

# California

## "I Have Found It"

CALIFORNIA REPUBLIC

★ **Sacramento**

North

0          100 Miles
0     100 Kilometers

# Colorado

## *"Nothing Without Providence"*

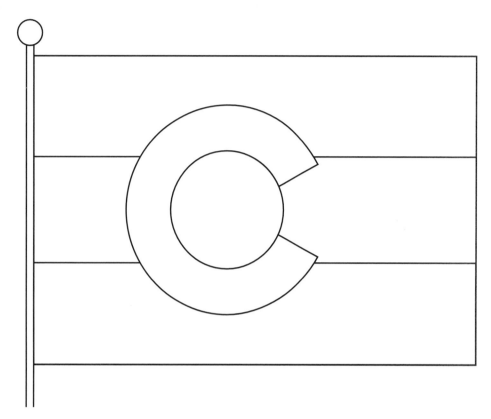

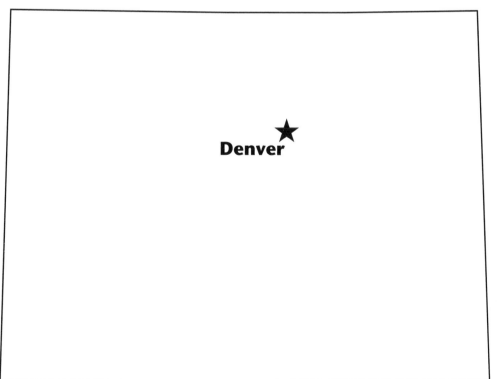

**Denver**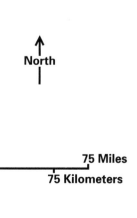

North

0         **75 Miles**
0       **75 Kilometers**

# Connecticut

## *"He Who Transplanted Still Sustains"*

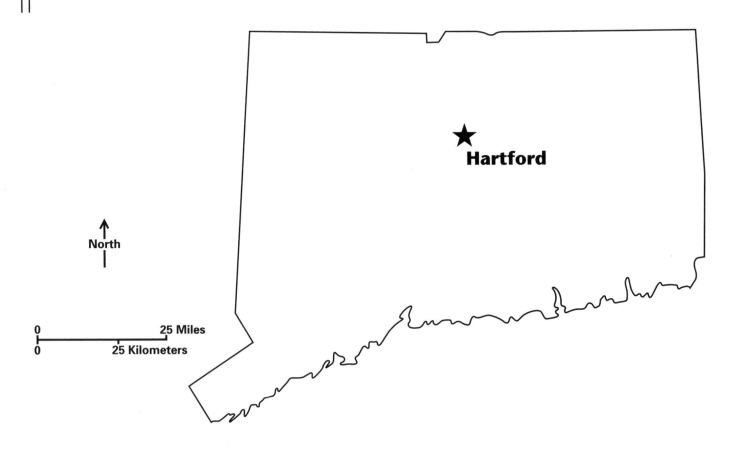

★
**Hartford**

North

0         25 Miles
0        25 Kilometers

# Delaware

## "Liberty and Independence"

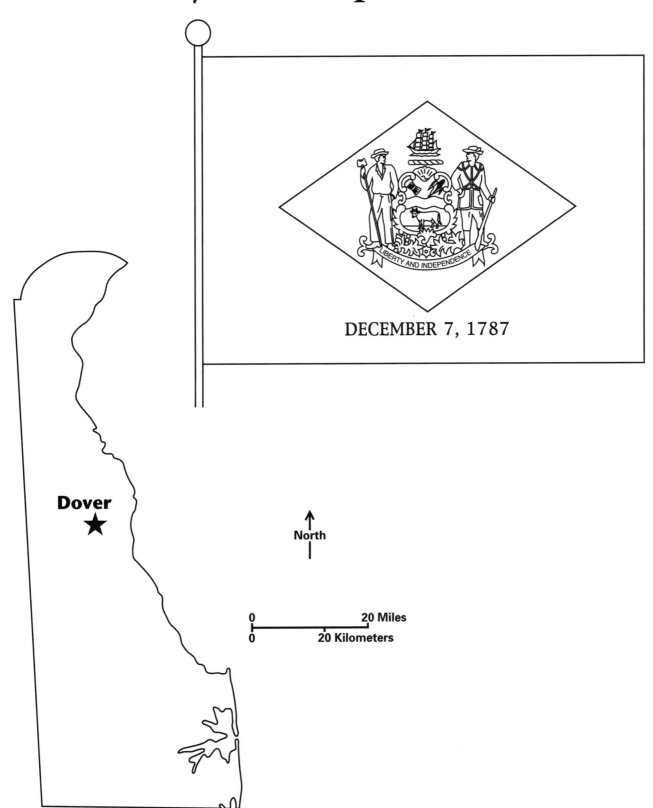

DECEMBER 7, 1787

Dover ★

↑
North

0            20 Miles

0            20 Kilometers

# Florida

## *"In God We Trust"*

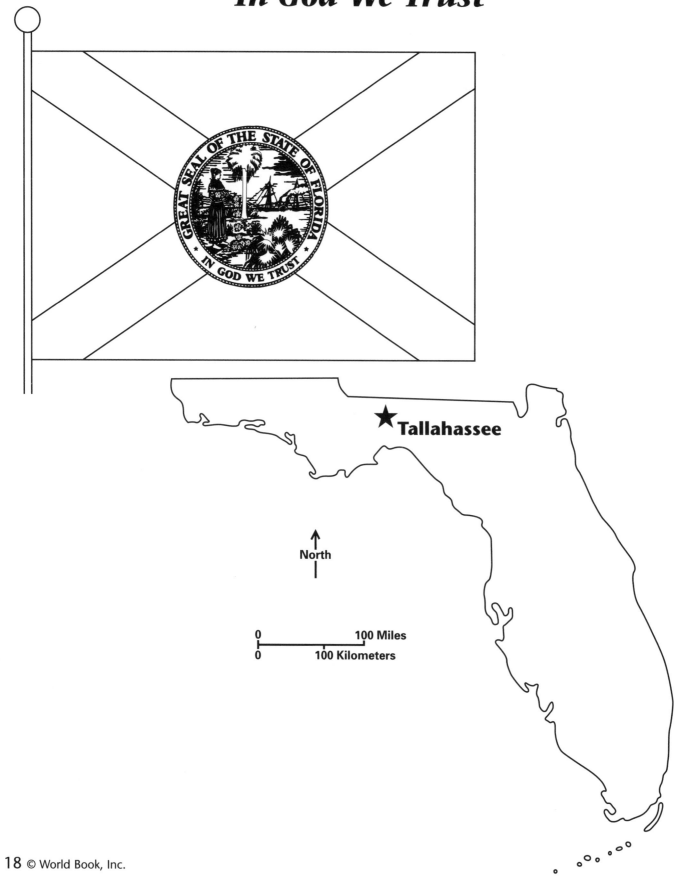

North

0         100 Miles

0         100 Kilometers

★ **Tallahassee**

# Georgia

*"Wisdom, Justice, and Moderation"*

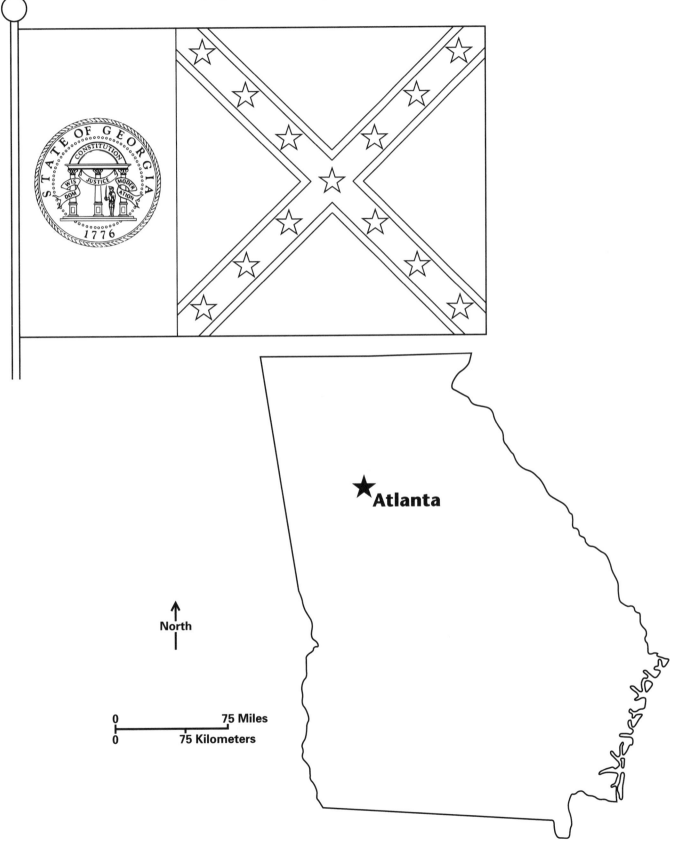

North

0          75 Miles
0        75 Kilometers

★Atlanta

# Hawaii

## *"The Life of the Land Is Perpetuated in Righteousness"*

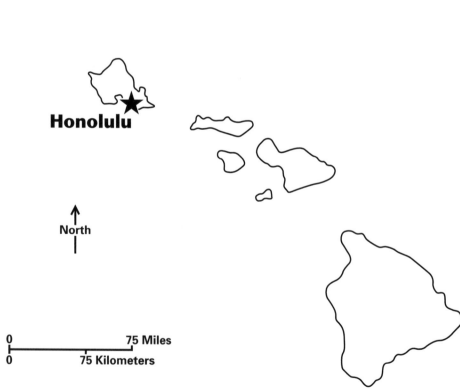

**Honolulu**

↑
**North**

0            **75 Miles**
0            **75 Kilometers**

# Idaho

## *"Let It Be Perpetual"*

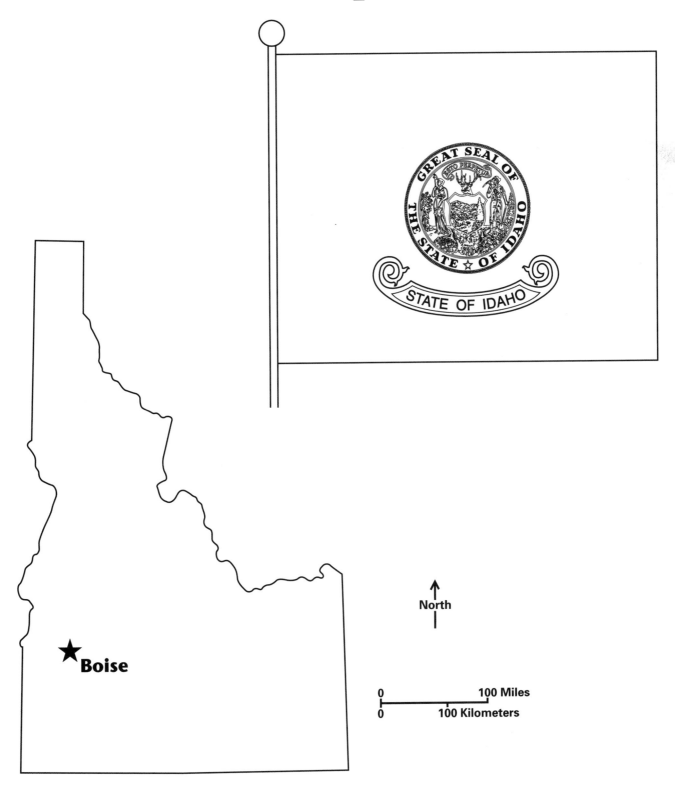

★**Boise**

North

0       100 Miles

0       100 Kilometers

# Illinois

## "State Sovereignty, National Union"

ILLINOIS

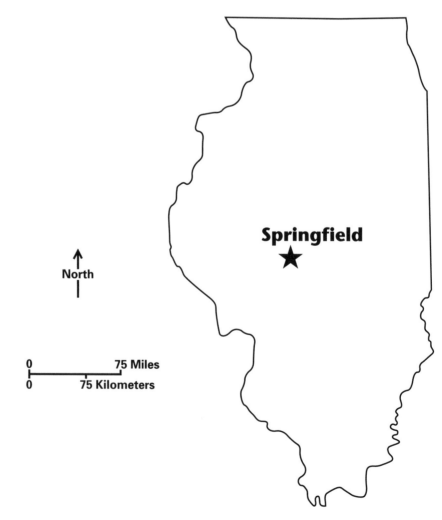

**Springfield**
★

North

0        75 Miles
0        75 Kilometers

# Indiana

## *"The Crossroads of America"*

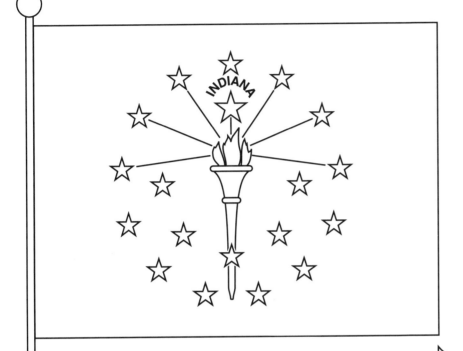

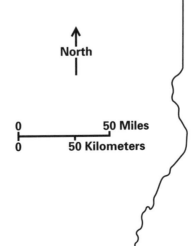

North

0       50 Miles
0       50 Kilometers

**Indianapolis**
★

# Iowa

## *"Our Liberties We Prize and Our Rights We Will Maintain"*

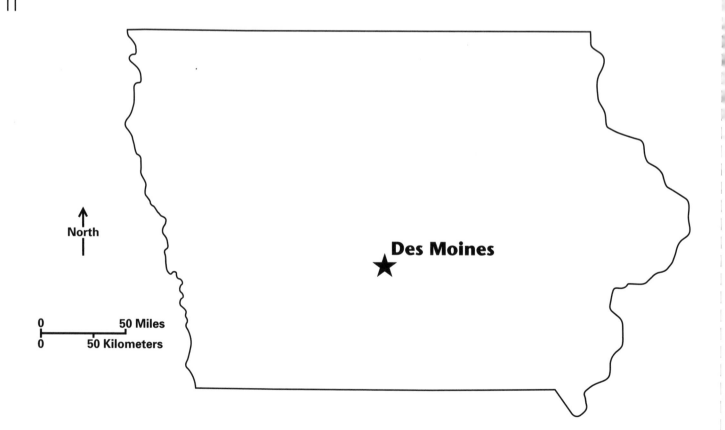

North

Des Moines

0        50 Miles
0    50 Kilometers

# Kansas

## *"To the Stars Through Difficulties"*

KANSAS

**North**

0   50 Miles
0   50 Kilometers

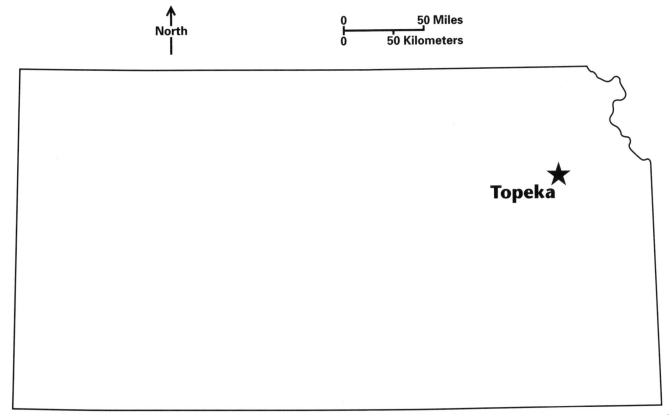

Topeka ★

# Kentucky

## *"United We Stand, Divided We Fall"*

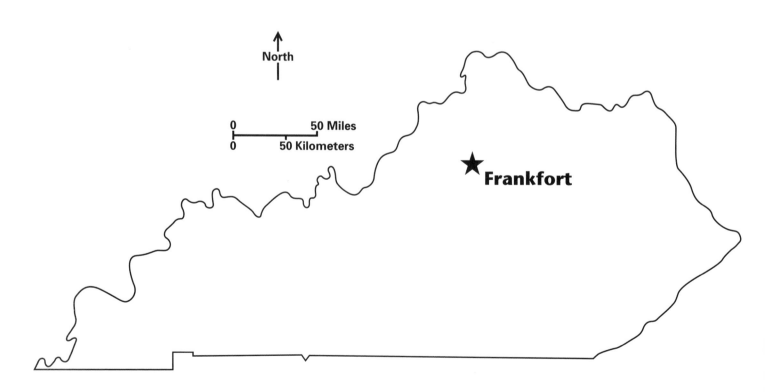

North

0          50 Miles

0          50 Kilometers

★ **Frankfort**

# Louisiana

## *"Union, Justice, and Confidence"*

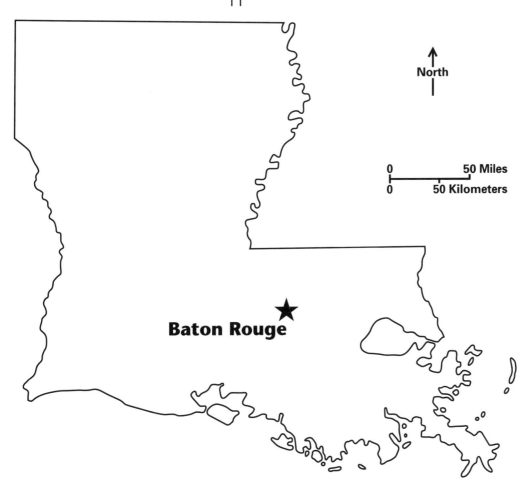

North

0       50 Miles

0       50 Kilometers

★ Baton Rouge

# Maine

## *"I Direct"* or *"I Guide"*

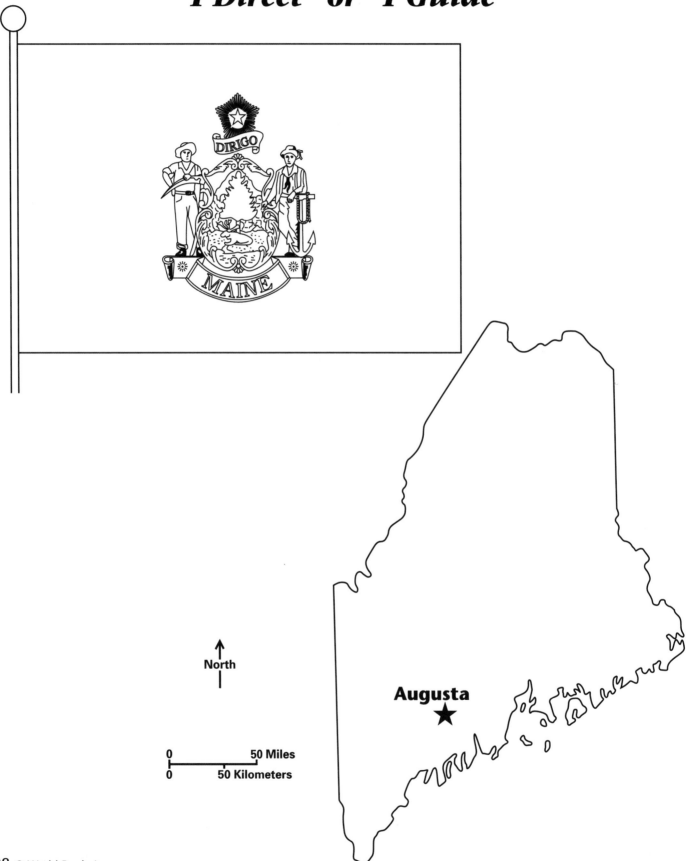

North

Augusta ★

0       50 Miles
0       50 Kilometers

# Maryland

## *"Manly Deeds, Womanly Words"*

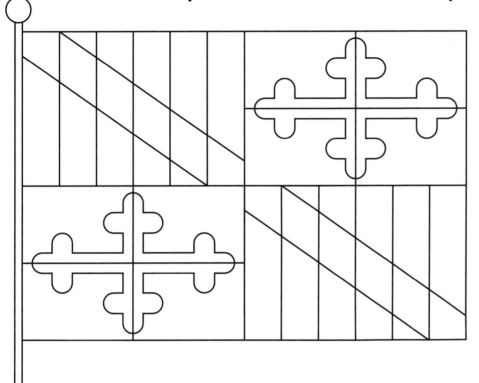

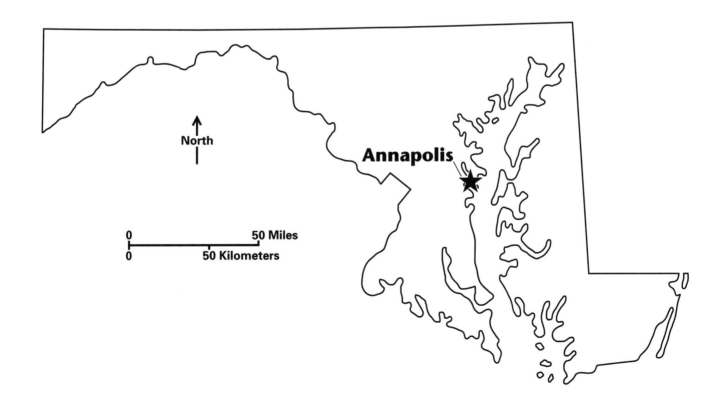

North

Annapolis

0 — 50 Miles
0 — 50 Kilometers

# Massachusetts

*"By the Sword We Seek Peace,*
*but Peace Only Under Liberty"*

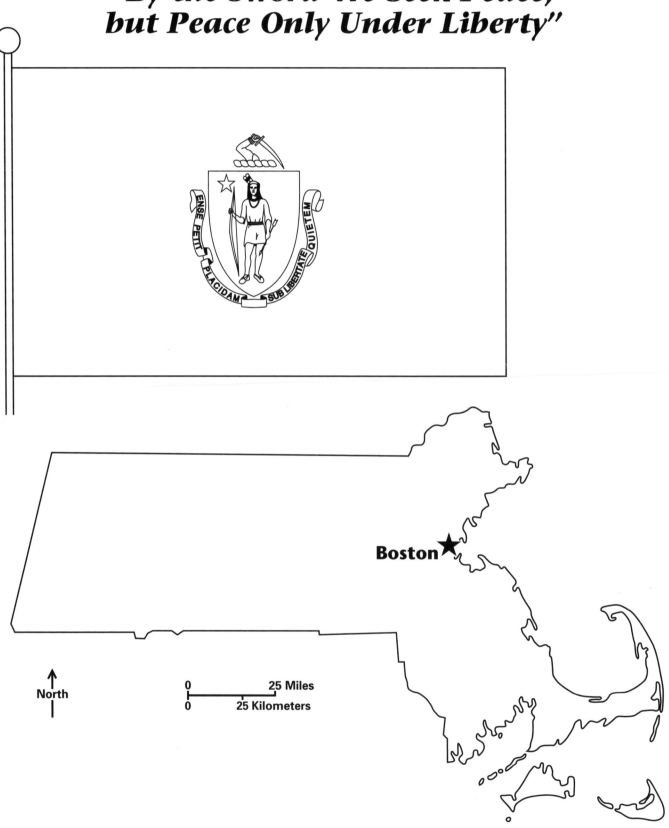

North

0       25 Miles
0       25 Kilometers

Boston ★

# Michigan

## "If You Seek a Pleasant Peninsula, Look About You"

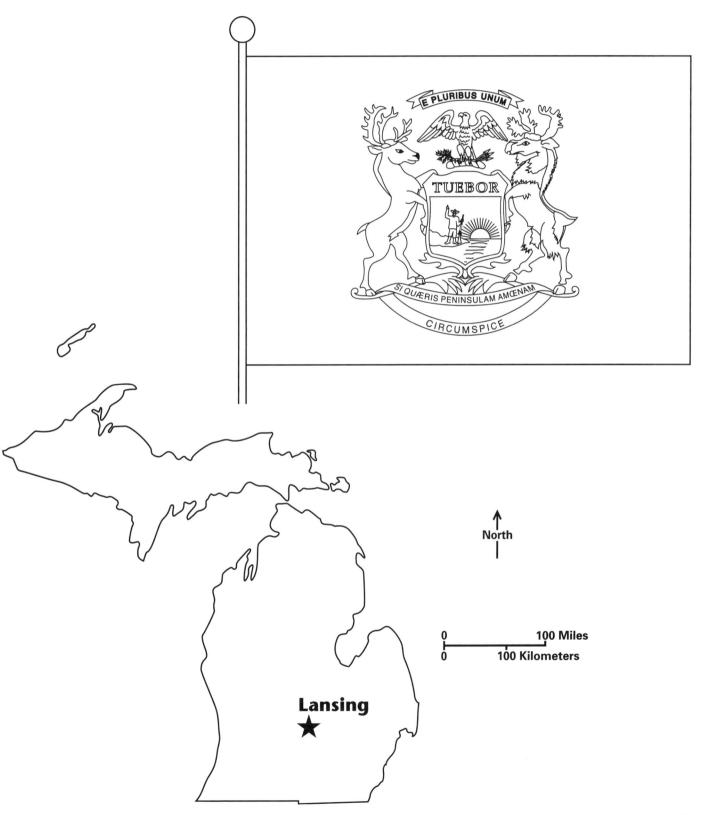

North

0          100 Miles
0          100 Kilometers

**Lansing**
★

# Minnesota

## *"The Star of the North"*

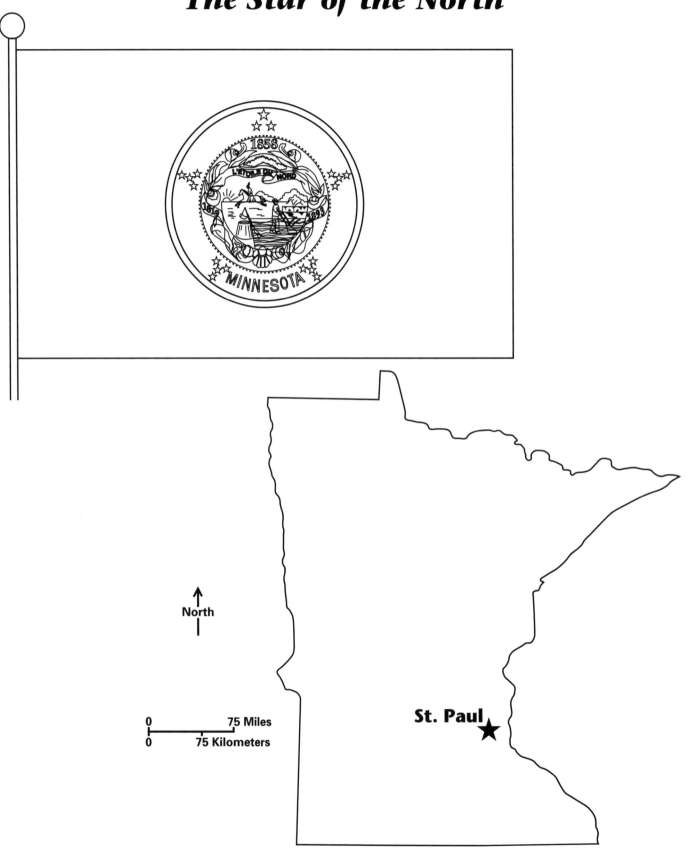

North

St. Paul ★

0         75 Miles
0      75 Kilometers

# Mississippi

## *"By Valor and Arms"*

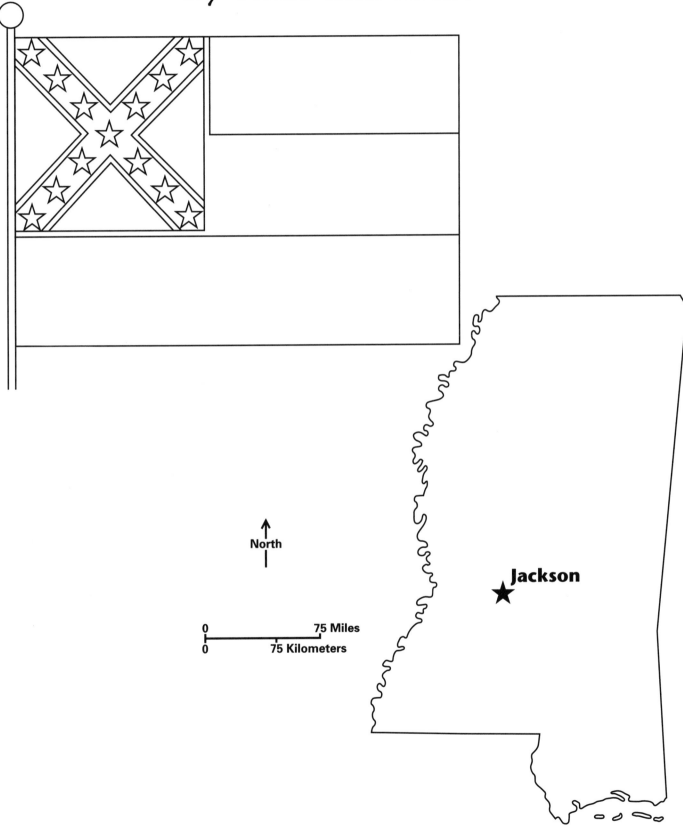

North

0          75 Miles
0          75 Kilometers

★ Jackson

# Missouri

## *"The Welfare of the People Shall Be the Supreme Law"*

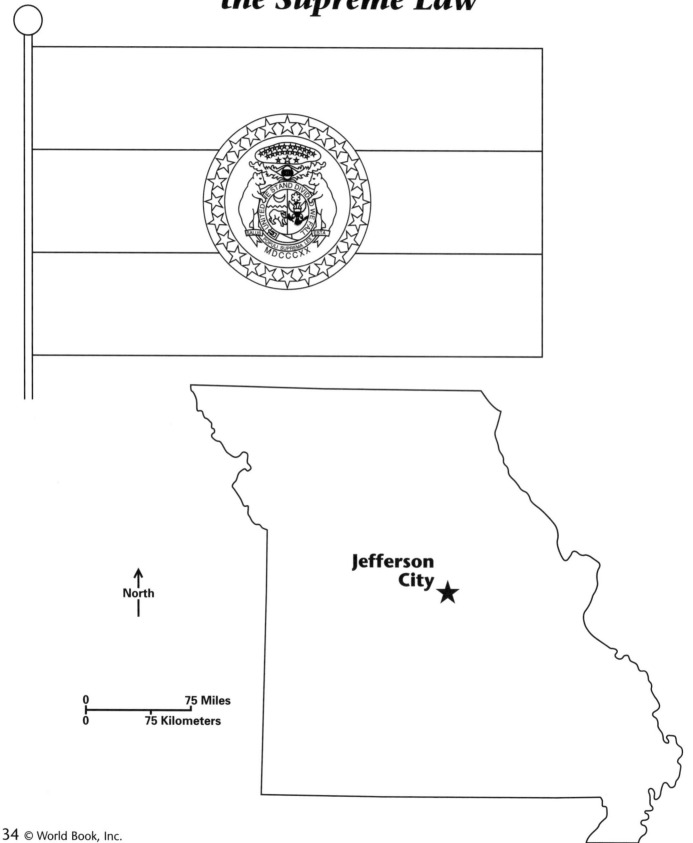

North

0          75 Miles
0          75 Kilometers

Jefferson City ★

# Montana

## *"Gold and Silver"*

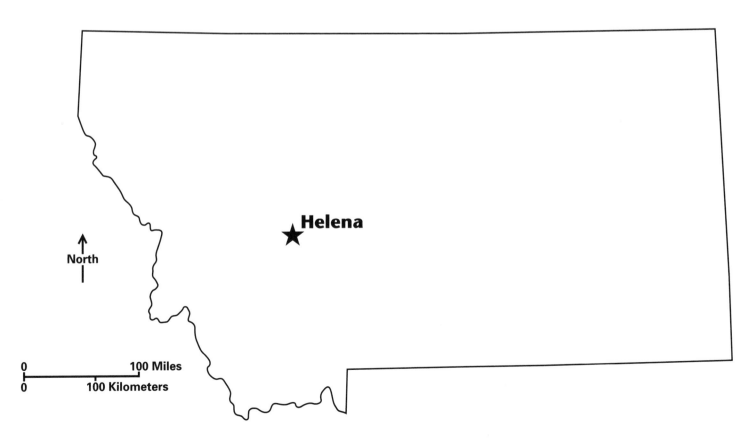

★ **Helena**

↑
**North**

0        100 Miles
0        100 Kilometers

# Nebraska

*"Equality Before the Law"*

**North**

0                75 Miles
0          75 Kilometers

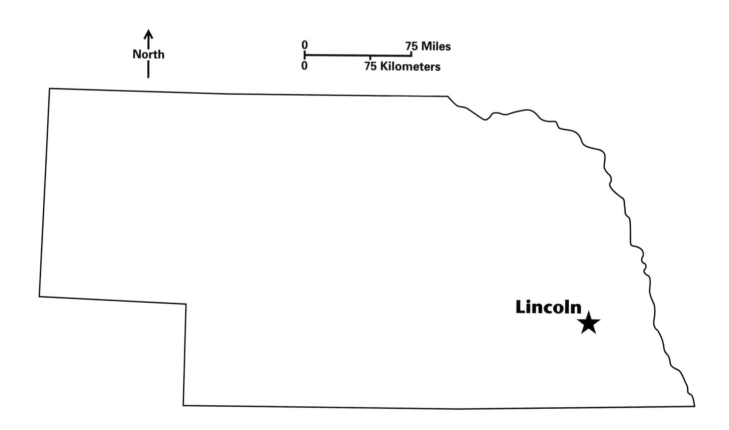

Lincoln ★

# Nevada

## *"All for Our Country"*

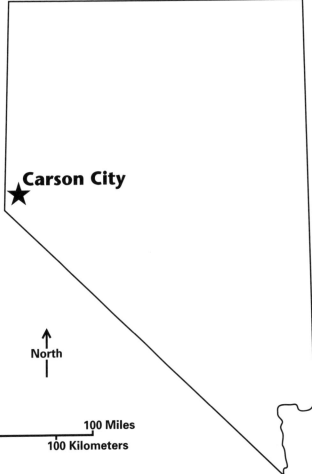

Carson City

↑
North

| 0 | 100 Miles |
| 0 | 100 Kilometers |

# New Hampshire

## *"Live Free or Die"*

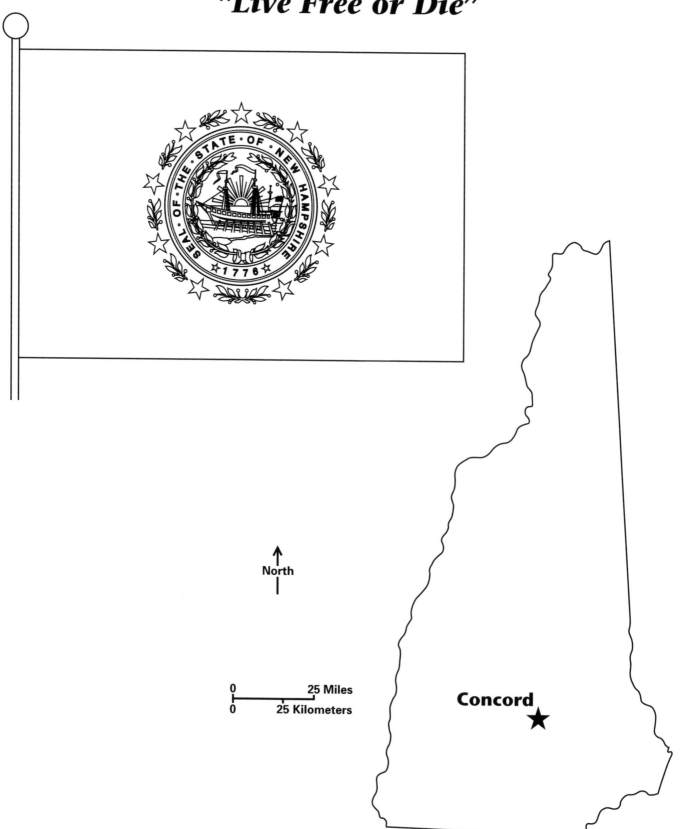

North

0 — 25 Miles
0 — 25 Kilometers

**Concord** ★

# New Jersey

## *"Liberty and Prosperity"*

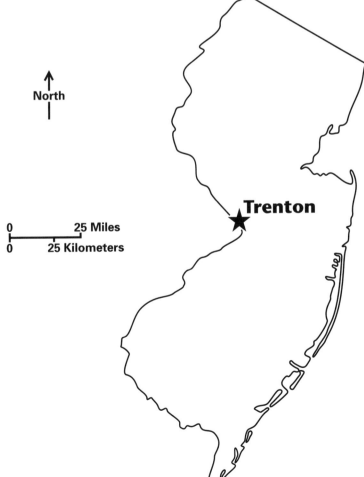

↑
**North**

0       25 Miles
0       25 Kilometers

★ **Trenton**

# New Mexico

## *"It Grows as It Goes"*

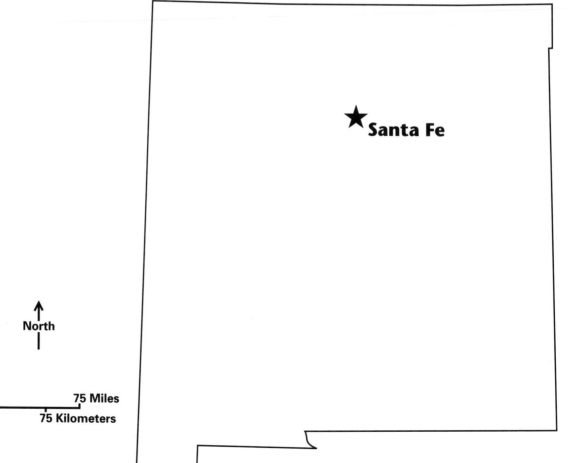

★ Santa Fe

North

```
0          75 Miles
0        75 Kilometers
```

# New York

*"Ever Upward"*

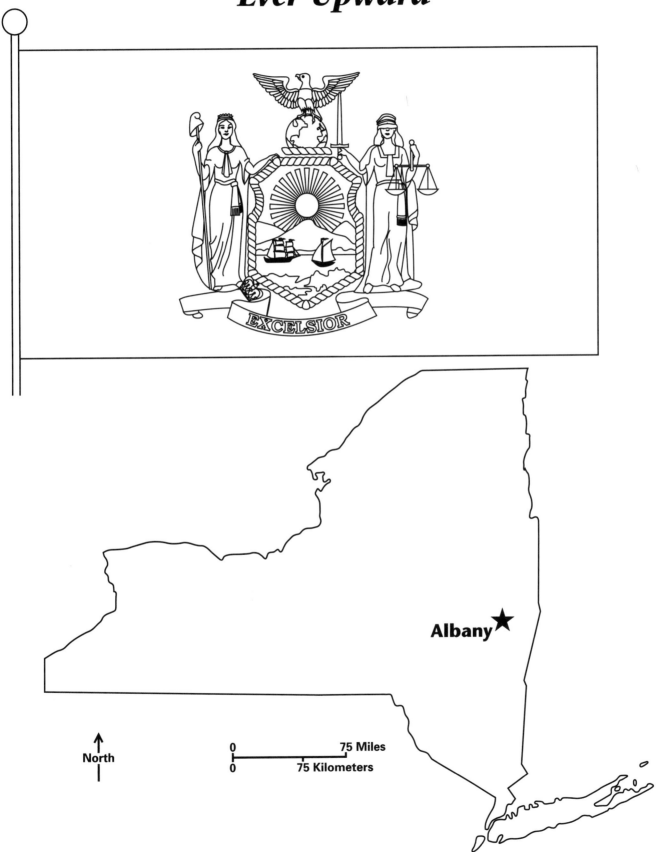

Albany ★

North

| 0 | | 75 Miles |
| 0 | | 75 Kilometers |

# North Carolina

*"To Be, Rather Than to Seem"*

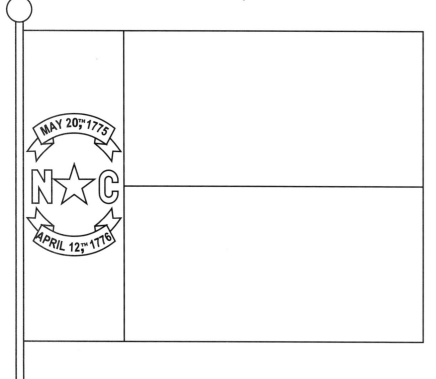

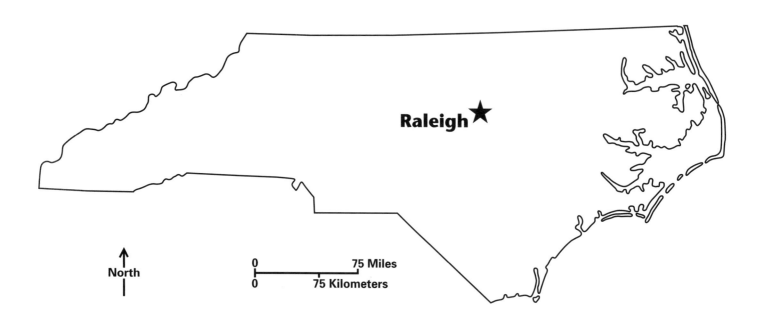

Raleigh ★

↑
North

0 _____ 75 Miles
0 _____ 75 Kilometers

# North Dakota

## *"Liberty and Union, Now and Forever, One and Inseparable"*

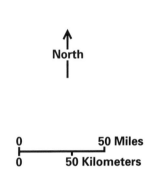

North

0          50 Miles

0          50 Kilometers

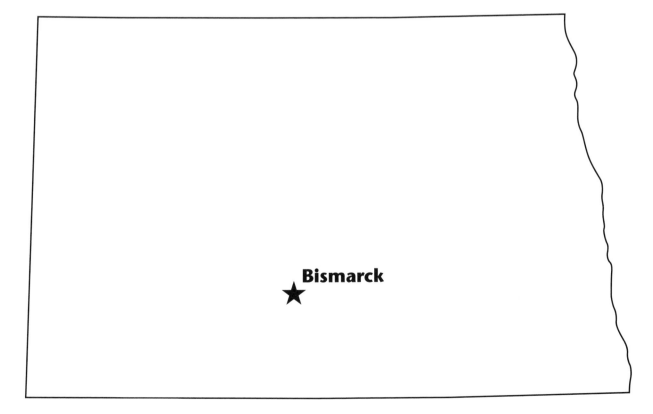

★ Bismarck

# Ohio

## *"With God, All Things Are Possible"*

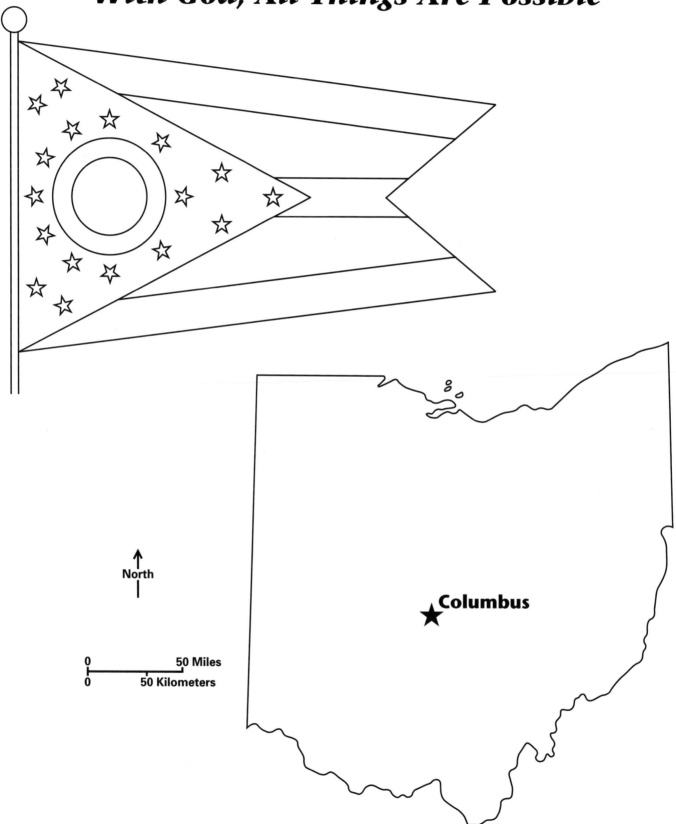

North

0          50 Miles
0        50 Kilometers

★ **Columbus**

# Oklahoma

*"Labor Conquers All Things"*

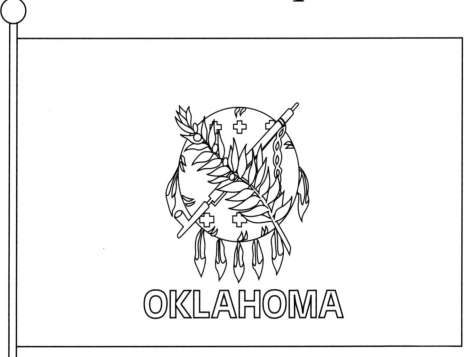

OKLAHOMA

North

Oklahoma
City

★

0        75 Miles
0     75 Kilometers

# Oregon

*"She Flies with Her Own Wings"*

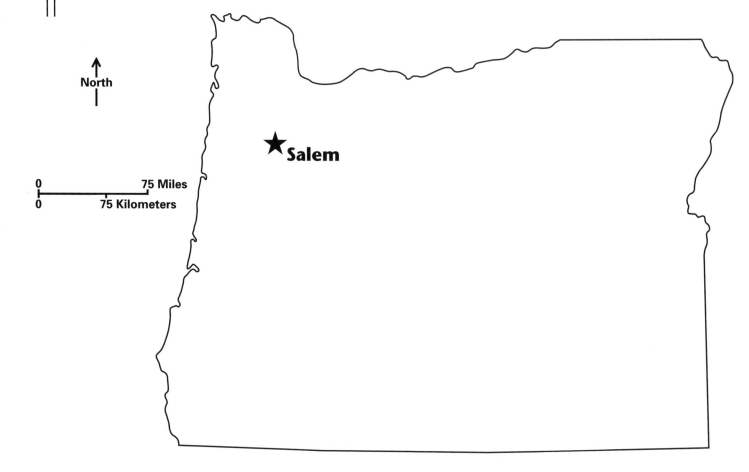

North

★ Salem

0          75 Miles
0         75 Kilometers

# Pennsylvania

## *"Virtue, Liberty, and Independence"*

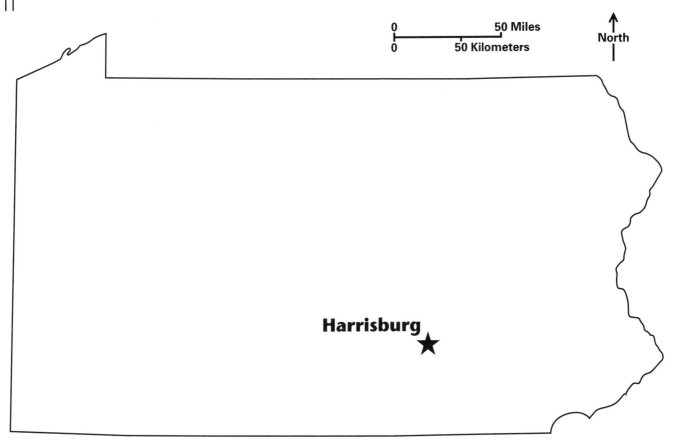

0    50 Miles

0    50 Kilometers

↑ North

**Harrisburg** ★

# Rhode Island

*"Hope"*

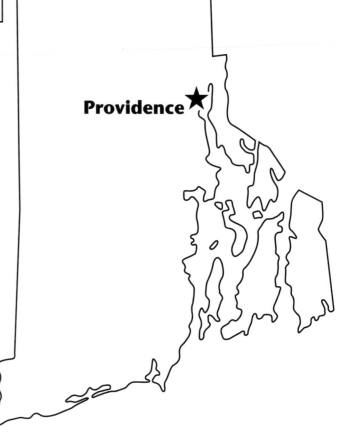

**Providence** ★

North

```
0                    10 Miles
0                    10 Kilometers
```

# South Carolina

*"Prepared in Mind and Resources"*
*and "While I Breathe, I Hope"*

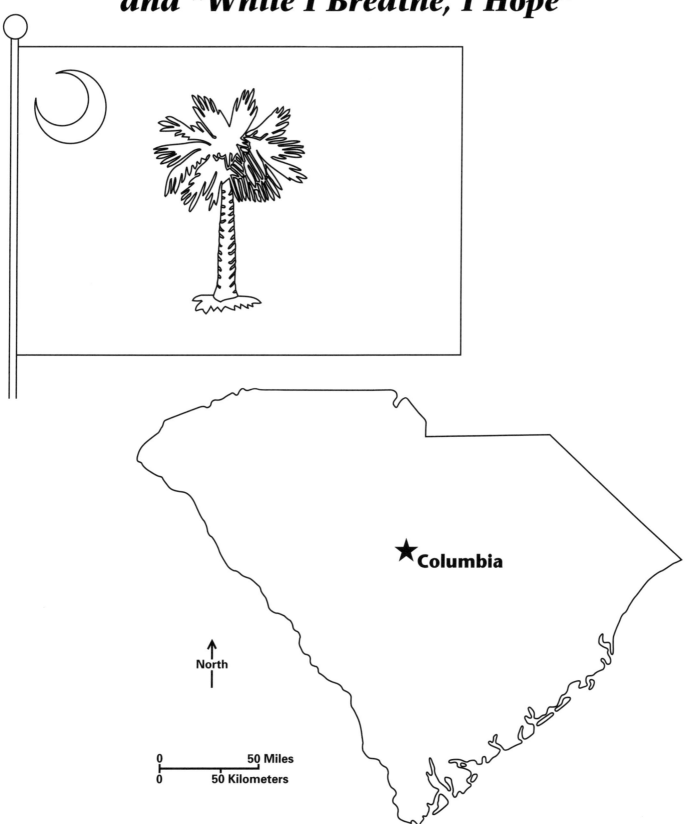

★ **Columbia**

↑
**North**

0         **50 Miles**
0     **50 Kilometers**

# South Dakota

*"Under God the People Rule"*

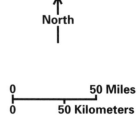

North

| 0 | 50 Miles |
|---|---|
| 0 | 50 Kilometers |

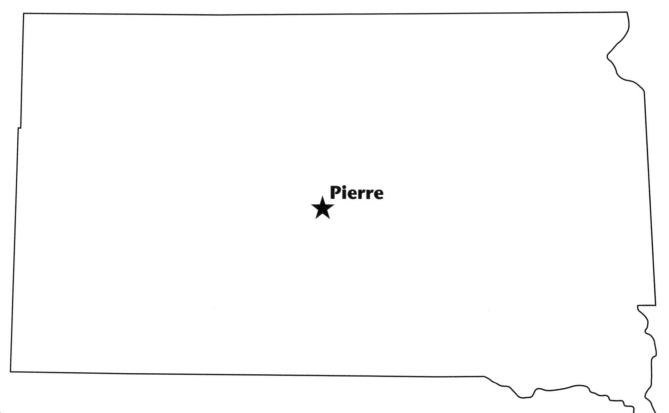

★ **Pierre**

© World Book, Inc.

# Tennessee

## *"Agriculture and Commerce"*

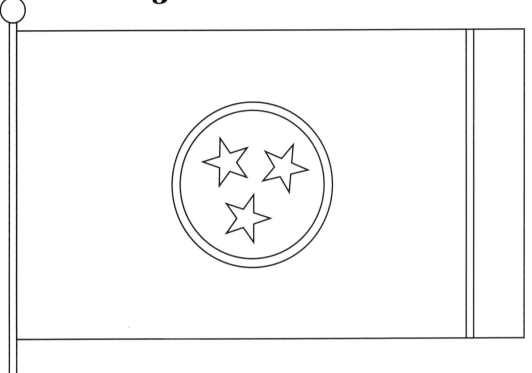

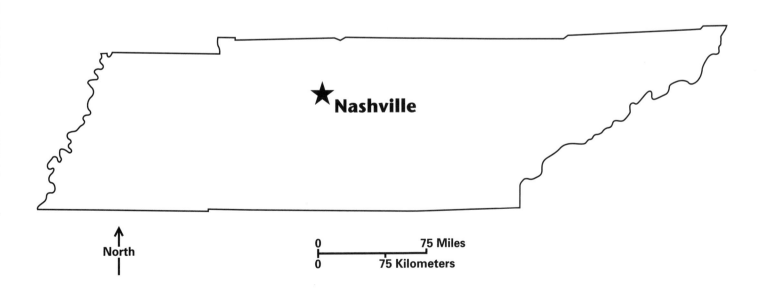

★ **Nashville**

**North**

0  75 Miles

0  75 Kilometers

# Texas

## *"Friendship"*

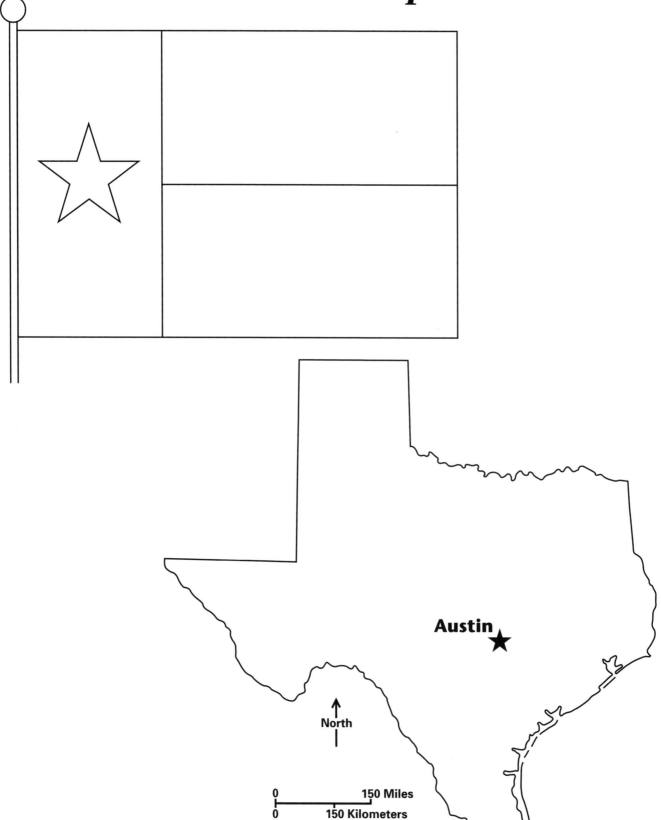

Austin ★

North

0        150 Miles
0        150 Kilometers

# Utah

*"Industry"*

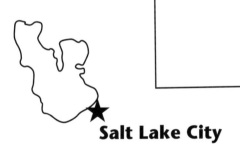

★ **Salt Lake City**

↑
North

| 0 | | 75 Miles |
| 0 | | 75 Kilometers |

# Vermont

## *"Freedom and Unity"*

North

0         25 Miles
0      25 Kilometers

★
**Montpelier**

# Virginia

## "Thus Always to Tyrants"

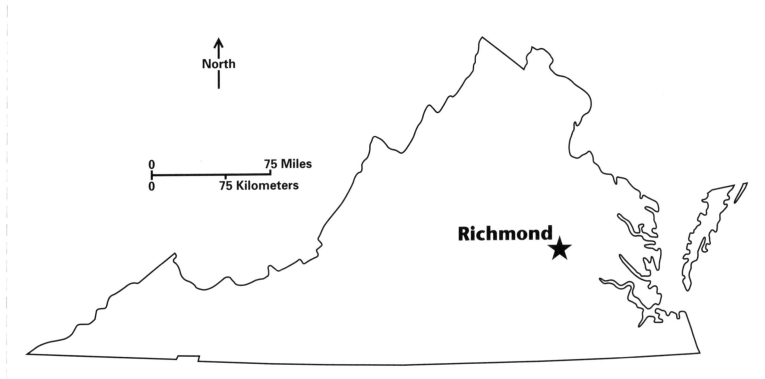

North

0          75 Miles
0          75 Kilometers

Richmond ★

# Washington

*"Bye and Bye"*

North

| 0 | 50 Miles |
|---|---|
| 0 | 50 Kilometers |

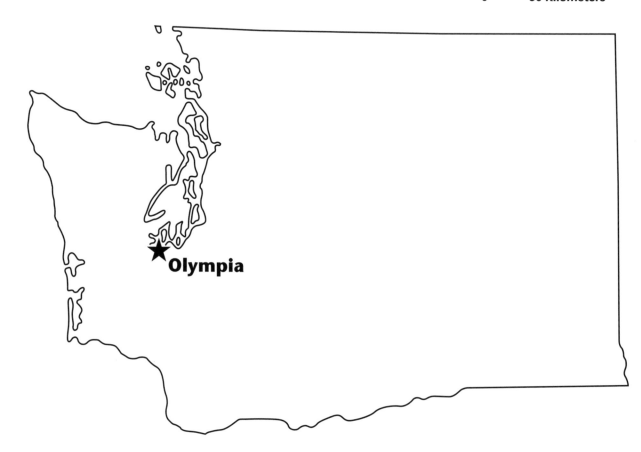

★ **Olympia**

# West Virginia

## *"Mountaineers Are Always Free"*

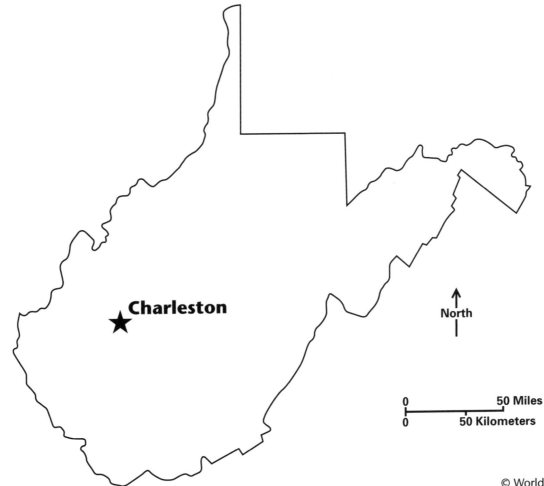

★ **Charleston**

North

0      50 Miles
0      50 Kilometers

# Wisconsin

## *"Forward"*

WISCONSIN

FORWARD

1848

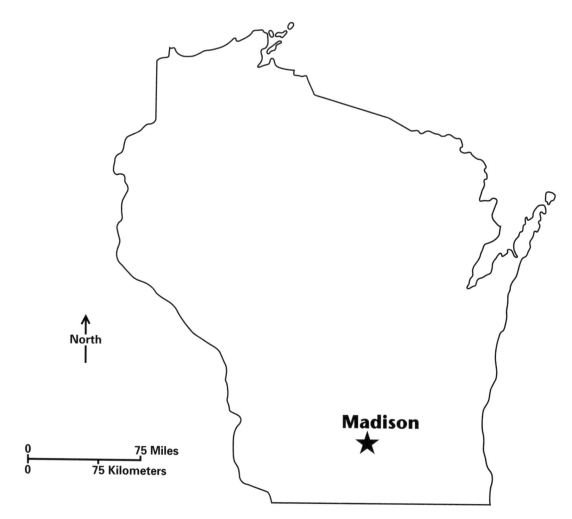

North

Madison

0          75 Miles
0          75 Kilometers

# Wyoming

*"Equal Rights"*

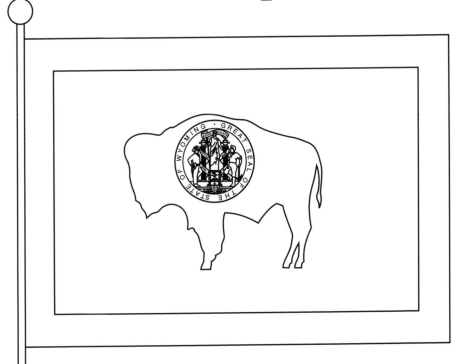

North

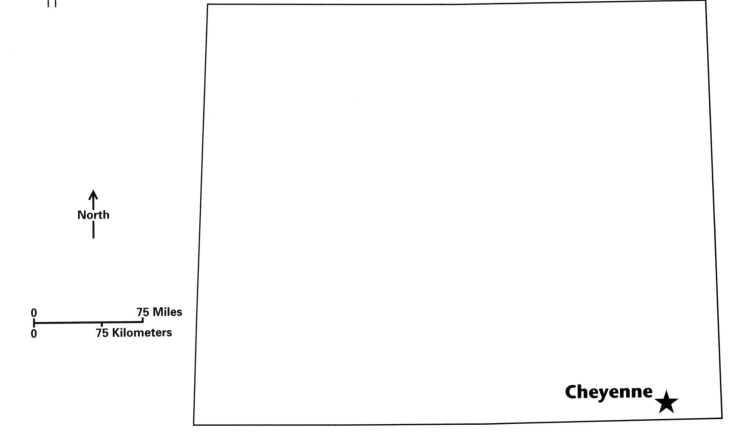

| 0 | | 75 Miles |
| 0 | 75 Kilometers | |

Cheyenne ★

# Word Search

## *States East of the Mississippi River*

Hidden in the letters below are the names of all the U.S. states east of the Mississippi River. Words may be hidden horizontally, vertically, or diagonally and may be forward or backward. One state is circled already to get you started. When you find the name of a state in the puzzle, circle it and cross it off the list.

```
K E A L S E R N U O H N E W J E R S E Y F P E
D N A L S I E D O H R T R E B N L E S A S C V
P I E E A X L I R R S W I S C O N S I N P C X
U A R W Z B W O N G A R S T P O N O O G H O R
B M A R Y L A N D A R H J V O E V U N M P P E
S I I P N O J M T D E S S I E A P T I S I O B
A S N C Y O R S A I P O A R B N T H L D R V E
P S I Y H E R K D R I N U G H O E C L A E P R
R I G N O I L E N O I A P I S M N A I R E E A
W S R M Z E G W F L M I E N Q U K R M C E N W
O S I W V S A A O F A M L I W O N O R I A N A
C I V B P H W R N T F I O A X E N L K I T S L
F P M A S S A C H U S E T T S T N I D U B Y E
M P R R E C D F I H R B Y K C U T N E K O L D
E I S D H J Y E V J O G E O R G I A A T V V M
M R T T E N N E S S E E N H R J B S K E I A O
E E R T N E W H A M P S H I R E K F E N J N O
M O R T T U C I T C E N N O C V N M R E E I P
N K L R D O J Y F R T J K S Y K M E R L I A O
```

| | | | | |
|---|---|---|---|---|
| Alabama | Illinois | Massachusetts | New York | South Carolina |
| Connecticut | Indiana | Michigan | North Carolina | Tennessee |
| Delaware | Kentucky | Mississippi | Ohio | ~~Vermont~~ |
| Florida | Maine | New Hampshire | Pennsylvania | Virginia |
| Georgia | Maryland | New Jersey | Rhode Island | West Virginia |
| | | | | Wisconsin |

# Word Search

## States West of the Mississippi River

Hidden in the letters below are the names of all the U.S. states west of the Mississippi River. Words may be hidden horizontally, vertically, or diagonally and may be forward or backward. One state is circled already to get you started. When you find the name of a state in the puzzle, circle it and cross it off the list.

```
A N W P S S E G I N B R E D V K L E I F O
R O D A R O L O C K C O N R M O E A D R P
S T R E S E C L W R E A I M C S P W B I A
A B X H M H E B P I S R M O H A K B M S A
R G T C A L I F O R N I A A Y S A X E T N
L L F W W K A N A E O Z R J E N H I O W A
G O A R I U N O G E R O N J O A M S D N I
N I T A B H E W A T N N E E L K E V A P S
I D O V Q U V U G N O A O N E N T I C E I
M A K S A L A P B K E N W R N R F H A T U
O H A O U S D A D V O W A I Y A U X G N O
Y O D A C M A N A T N O M B A N E A K A L
W M H K S O L N E T I T L E B I O J M R V
J O T C O I W E D B S P I L X R T O E K R
E F U D P A S T Y U R E W D H I H I S A E
W R O N H G C T A I M A I U O A C S J N S
M I S S O U R I E M R Z S O L H I O N S Z
U P E F O C G L U A L U E K P U H U F A I
I K Y E N O R T H D A K O T A N E Q Y S A
```

| | | | | |
|---|---|---|---|---|
| Alaska | Hawaii | Minnesota | New Mexico | Texas |
| Arizona | Idaho | Missouri | North Dakota | Utah |
| Arkansas | Iowa | Montana | Oklahoma | Washington |
| California | Kansas | ~~Nebraska~~ | Oregon | Wyoming |
| Colorado | Louisiana | Nevada | South Dakota | |

0
0
500 Miles
500 Kilometers

North

# Canada

## "From Sea to Sea"

Ottawa

# Canada Facts and Symbols

The flag of Canada features a red, 11-pointed maple leaf, a national symbol of the country. It became Canada's official flag in 1965.

The beaver, found in the northern part of the world, is also a national symbol of Canada.

The Canadian coat of arms includes three red maple leaves below the royal arms of England, Scotland, Ireland, and France.

Canada is the second largest country in the world, but the 36th in population.

Canada consists of 10 provinces and 3 territories. The country's capital is the city of Ottawa in the province of Ontario.

65

# Province/Territory Facts

| Provinces | Area in sq. mi. | Area in sq. km | Date became province |
|---|---|---|---|
| Alberta | 255,287 | 661,190 | 1905 |
| British Columbia | 365,900 | 947,800 | 1871 |
| Manitoba | 250,947 | 649,950 | 1870 |
| New Brunswick | 28,355 | 73,440 | 1867 |
| Newfoundland | 156,649 | 405,720 | 1949 |
| Nova Scotia | 21,423 | 55,490 | 1867 |
| Ontario | 412,581 | 1,068,580 | 1867 |
| Prince Edward Island | 2,185 | 5,660 | 1873 |
| Quebec | 594,860 | 1,540,680 | 1867 |
| Saskatchewan | 251,866 | 652,330 | 1905 |

| Territories | Area in sq. mi. | Area in sq. km | Date became territory |
|---|---|---|---|
| Northwest Territories | 501,570 | 1,299,070 | 1870 |
| Nunavut | 770,000 | 1,900,000 | 1999 |
| Yukon Territory | 186,661 | 483,450 | 1898 |

# Alberta

## *"Strong and Free"*

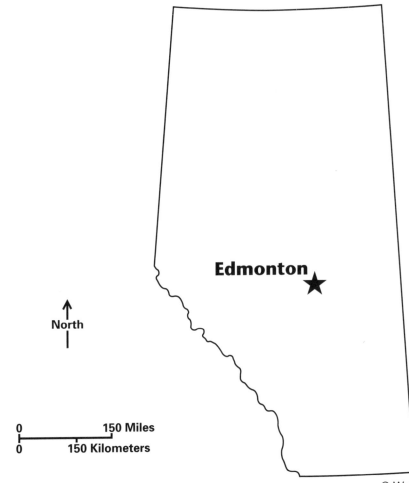

Edmonton ★

North

0         150 Miles
0        150 Kilometers

# British Columbia

## *"Splendor Without Diminishment"*

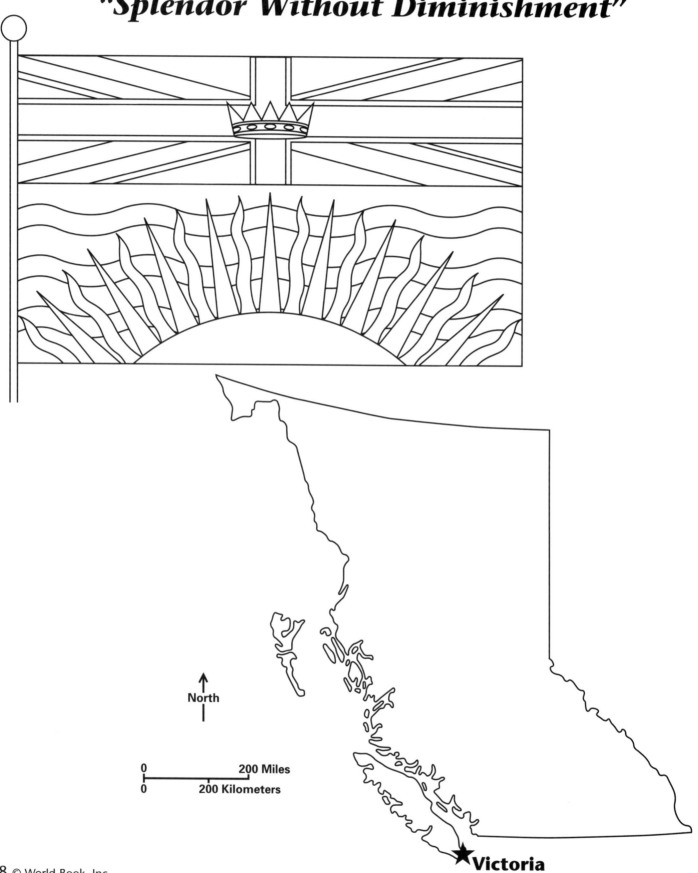

North

| 0 | | 200 Miles |
| 0 | | 200 Kilometers |

★ Victoria

# Manitoba

## *(no motto)*

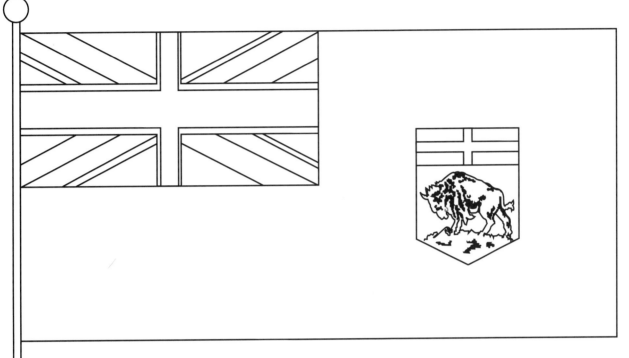

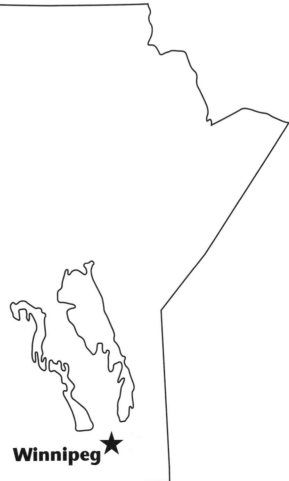

North

0           150 Miles
0        150 Kilometers

**Winnipeg** ★

# New Brunswick

## *"Hope Restored"*

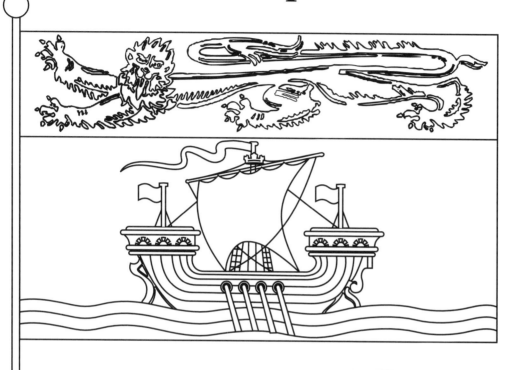

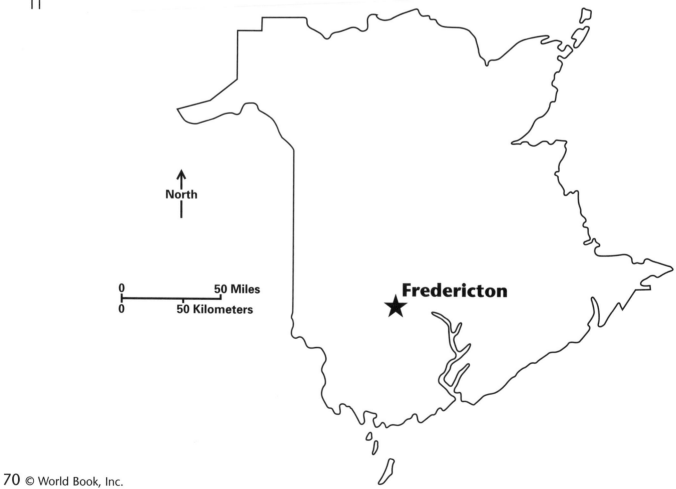

North

0 — 50 Miles
0 — 50 Kilometers

★ **Fredericton**

# Newfoundland

## *"Seek Ye First the Kingdom of God"*

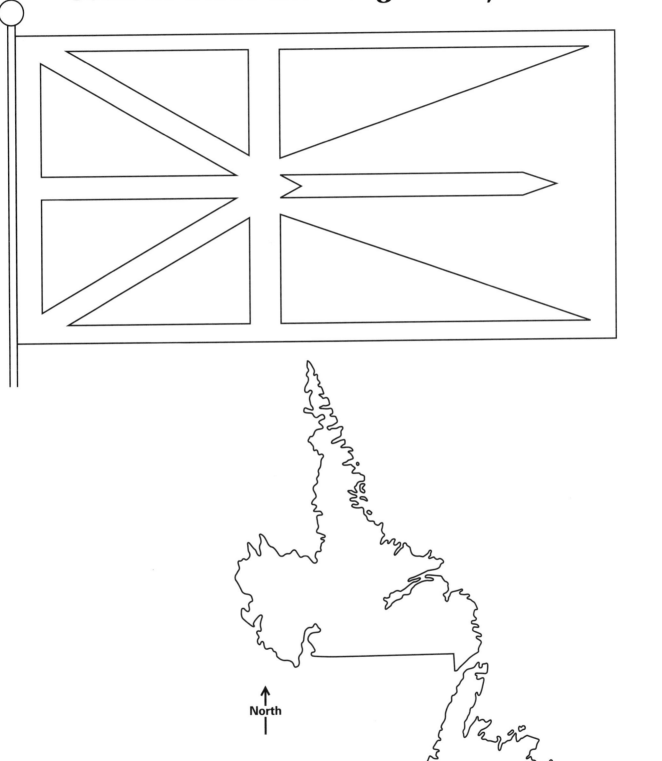

North

0       200 Miles
0       200 Kilometers

★ St. John's

# Northwest Territories

*(no motto)*

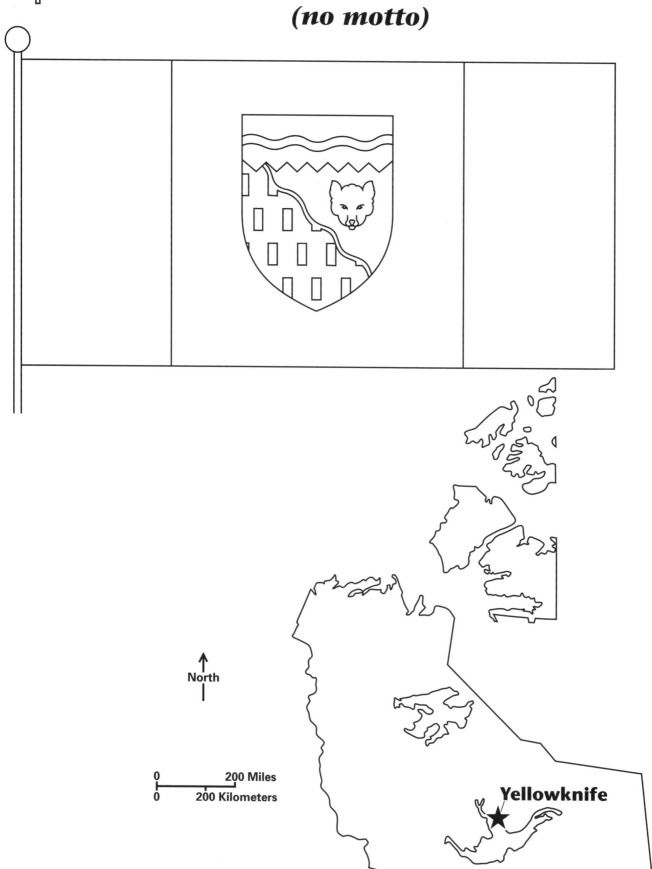

North

0      200 Miles
0      200 Kilometers

★ Yellowknife

# Nova Scotia

*"One Defends and the Other Conquers"*

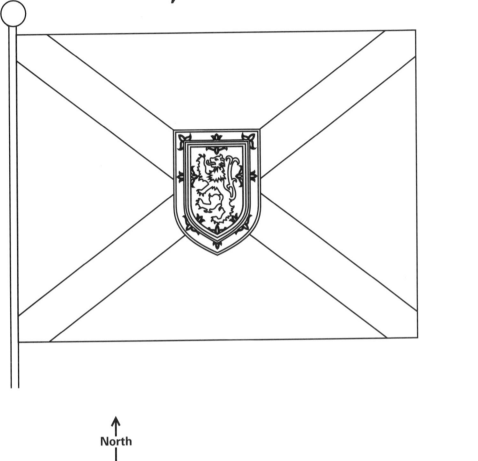

North

0       50 Miles

0       50 Kilometers

**Halifax** ★

# Nunavut

*(no motto)*

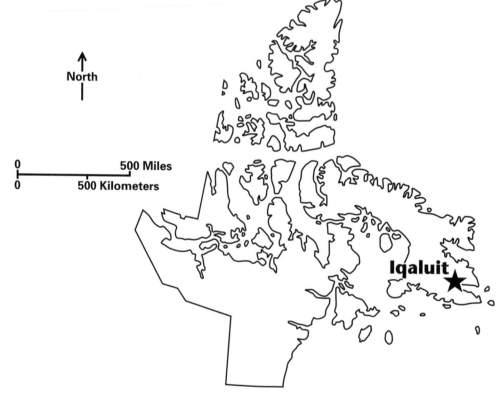

North

| 0 | | 500 Miles |
| 0 | | 500 Kilometers |

Iqaluit ★

# Ontario

*"Loyal She Began, Loyal She Remains"*

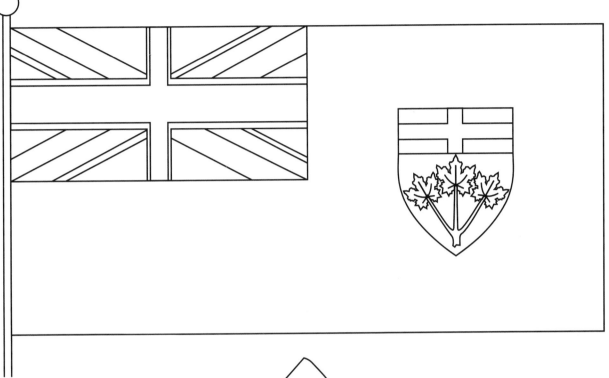

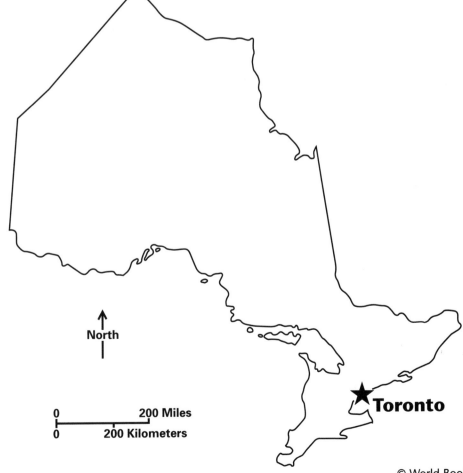

North

| 0 | 200 Miles |
| 0 | 200 Kilometers |

★ Toronto

# Prince Edward Island

## "The Small Under the Protection of the Great"

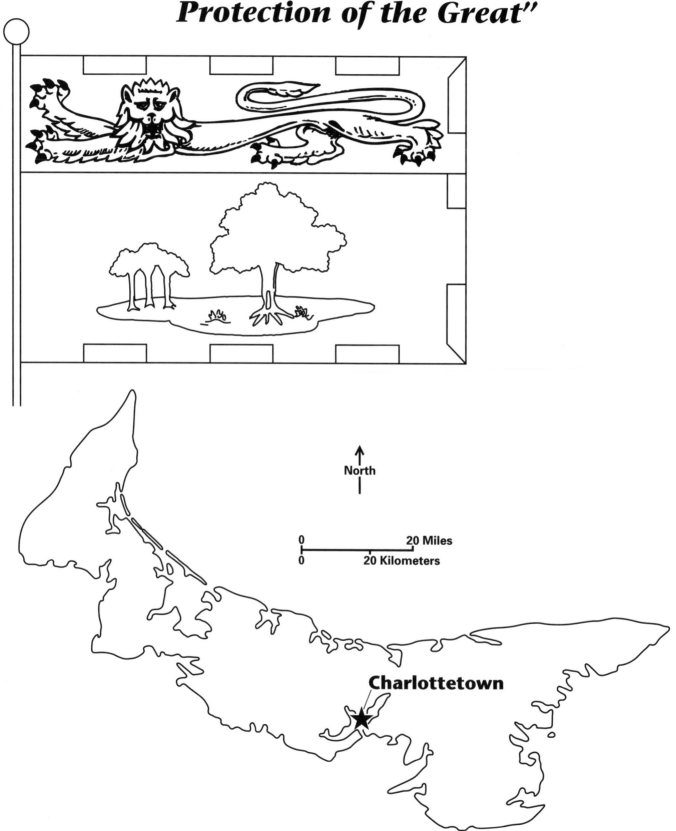

North

0            20 Miles
0            20 Kilometers

**Charlottetown**

# Quebec

## *"I Remember"*

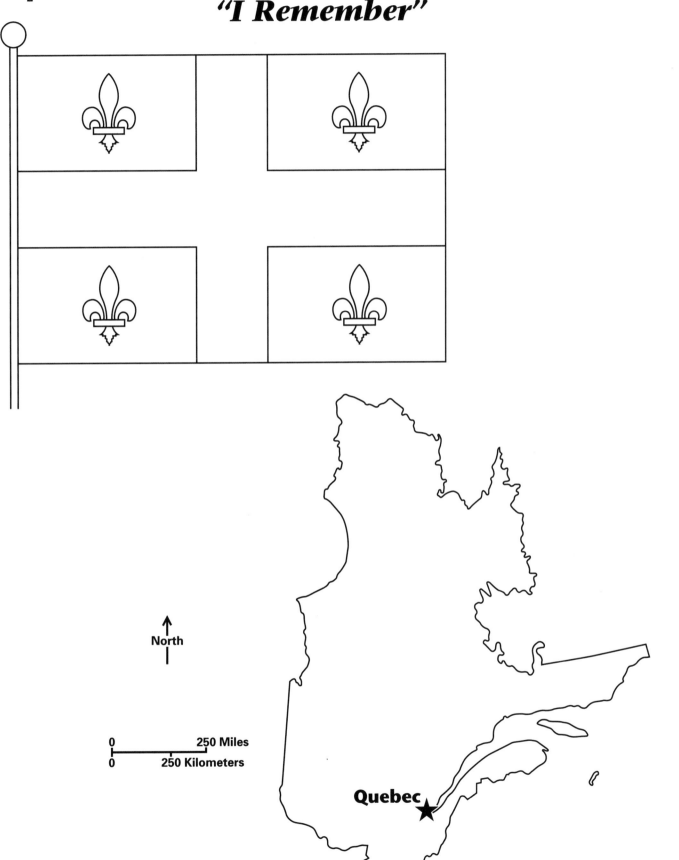

North

0        250 Miles
0        250 Kilometers

**Quebec** ★

# Saskatchewan

## *"From Many Peoples Strength"*

North

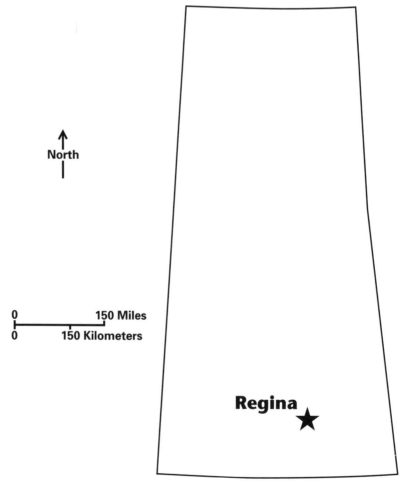

0 — 150 Miles
0 — 150 Kilometers

**Regina** ★

# Yukon Territory

## *(no motto)*

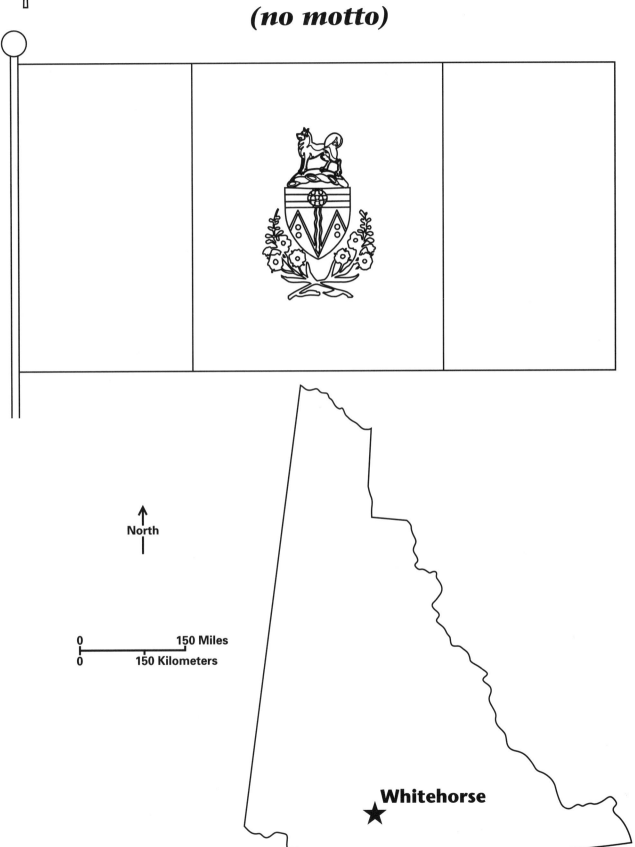

North

0 — 150 Miles
0 — 150 Kilometers

★ **Whitehorse**

# Crossword Puzzle

## Provinces and Territories

**ACROSS**

1. Which province has the capital of Winnipeg?
3. Which part of Canada is the farthest south?
6. Which part of Canada has the capital of Halifax?
8. Which province comes first alphabetically?
10. Which part of Canada has the longest name?
11. Which province is the farthest east?
12. Which province has the capital of Fredericton?

**DOWN**

2. Which province is on the Pacific coast?
4. Which part of Canada is the farthest west?
5. Which is the smallest province?
7. Which province is made of four straight sides?
9. Which part of Canada has the shortest name?
10. Which part of Canada has the most islands?